VIOLINJUDY'S
LANE'S SUMMER

SUPPLEMENTARY SONGS AND ACTIVITIES
FOR BEGINNING VIOLIN STUDENTS

Violin Judy's

VERY FUN VIOLIN COLLECTION

Lane's Summer by Judy Naillon
Copyright   ©2023 ViolinJudy
www.violinjudy.com
ISBN: 978-1-960674-22-7

Violin Judy's

VERY FUN VIOLIN LIBRARY

LEVEL B

Lane's Summer is composed for violin students in levelB. Learners using this book should be able to hold the instrument up in playing position, understand a basic bow grip and have experience playing with fingers on the violin. A book level chart for the *Very Fun Violin Collection* is provided at the end of this book.

LANE IS HAVING A TOUGH SUMMER. HE WANTS TO PLAY VIDEO GAMES BUT MOM SIGNED HIM UP FOR STUFF TO DO AND IT'S NOT. FUN. AT. ALL!

NOTE TO TEACHERS/PRACTICE PARENT:

Any beginning Violin Student can start in this book on a real instrument. For a total beginner *A Violin Twinkle A* will be a more helpful book to start! The pacing of this series is slower than any other method book you will find. This allows younger beginners time to really learn to read music as well as play a wide variety of songs. When you establish a firm foundation of technic, listening skills and songs students know and like to play, you'll have a violinist who learns to love music! Playing pieces that are traditional and familiar, yet presented in a fun, fresh way engages the learner.

We start with notes on the A string and later add only open E. The pacing is graded in a manner that the note reading will not be overwhelming and the note heads are large and carefully placed to aid in tracking-reading from top to bottom and left to right. The advantage of having a printed book to send home with learners helps everyone remember what and how to practice and even young children are often able to practice these without help after the first few lessons. You may use this book with any other Violin learning method.

In this book you will find many
tools to help your students learn the Violin including
FUN songs and worksheets!

Pieces in this book are fun to play in group lessons as well!
Students who have successfully completed this book can look forward to more skills to learn and fun pieces to master in *A Very Fun Violin Collection* available on Amazon

DO`S AND DON`TS FOR VIOLIN:

WASH YOUR HANDS BEFORE YOU PLAY OR PRACTICE VIOLIN.

PLACE YOUR MUSIC ON THE STAND BEFORE YOU OPEN YOUR VIOLIN CASE.

HOLD YOUR BOW WITH THE FROG OR STICK. AVOID TOUCHING THE HAIR. NATURAL OILS ON CLEAN HANDS CAN RUB OFF ON YOUR BOW WHICH PREVENTS ROSIN FROM STICKING TO YOUR BOW.

WHEN TUNING YOUR VIOLIN USE THE FINE TUNERS FOR SMALL PITCH CHANGES.

REMEMBER RIGHTY TIGHTY FOR THE PITCH TO GO HIGHER AND LEFTY LOOSEY FOR

THE PITCH TO GO LOWER.

DON`T LET YOUR VIOLIN "WIGGLE" BACK AND FORTH WHEN YOU PLAY. YOUR VIOLIN SHOULD STAY STILL AND FLAT AS A TABLETOP. THE VIOLIN IS THE CONSTANT AND THE BOW IS THE VARIABLE.

ROSIN YOUR BOW A LOT WHEN IT`S BRAND NEW. IN THE FUTURE, JUST THREE SWIPES UP AND DOWN BEFORE YOU PRACTICE EACH DAY IS ENOUGH.

DON`T HOLD YOUR BOW LIKE THIS:

DO USE A MUSIC STAND!
IT WILL HELP YOU HOLD YOUR VIOLIN
CORRECTLY-FLAT LIKE A TABLE AND
YOU`LL SOUND BETTER!

WHOLE NOTE	HALF NOTE	QUARTER NOTE	EIGHTH NOTES

"WHOLE NOTE HOLD IT" 4 BEATS	"HOLD ME" 2 BEATS	"QUARTER" 1 BEAT	TWO 8TH NOTES = 1 QUARTER NOTE

FERMATA	SHARP	FLAT	TREBLE CLEF

HOLD NOTES LONGER THAN NORMAL	RAISE PITCH BY A HALF STEP	LOWER PITCH BY A HALF STEP	G CLEF TREBLE NOTES

WHOLE REST	HALF REST	QUARTER REST	REPEAT SIGN

HOLD 4 BEATS	HOLD 2 BEATS	HOLD 1 BEAT	PLAY AGAIN

DOUBLE BAR LINE	STAFF	BAR LINE	DOTTED HALF NOTE
			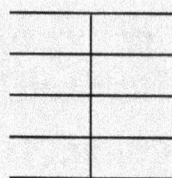
THE END OF THE PIECE	5 LINES 4 SPACES	DIVIDES STAFF INTO MEASURES	"HOLD ME PLEASE" THREE BEATS

PARTS OF THE VIOLIN

Sing the Parts of the Violin with your Teacher in a G scale! This is the Scroll, These are the Pegs, This is the Nut...

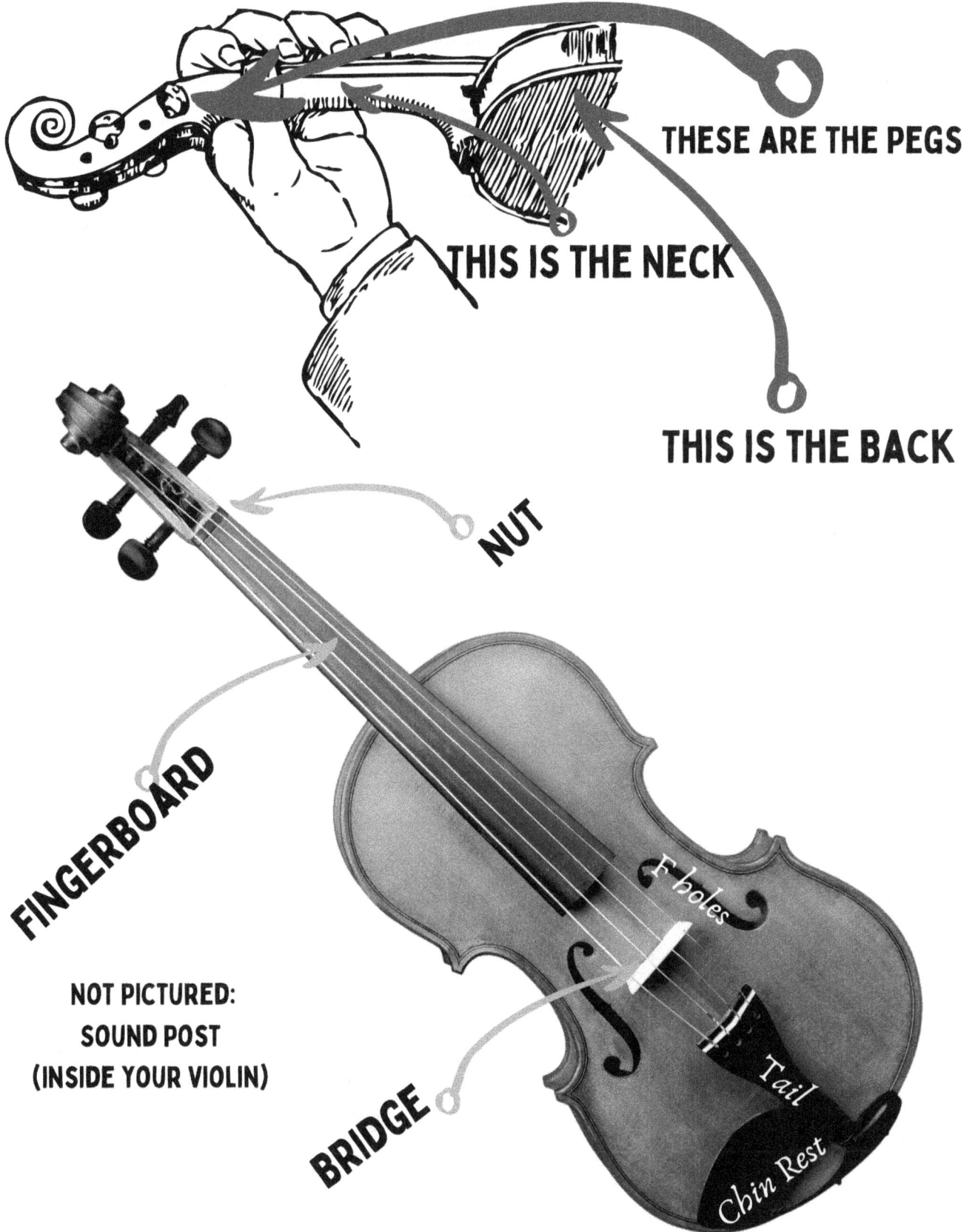

THESE ARE THE PEGS

THIS IS THE NECK

THIS IS THE BACK

NUT

FINGERBOARD

NOT PICTURED:
SOUND POST
(INSIDE YOUR VIOLIN)

F holes

Tail

Chin Rest

BRIDGE

TREBLE CLEF LINE & SPACE NOTES

DRAW TREBLE CLEF LINE & SPACE NOTES

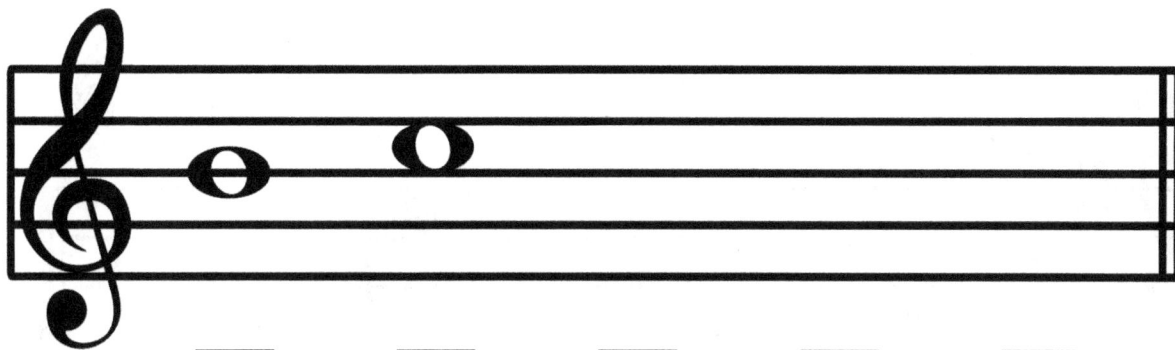

L   S   S   L   L

S   L   S   L

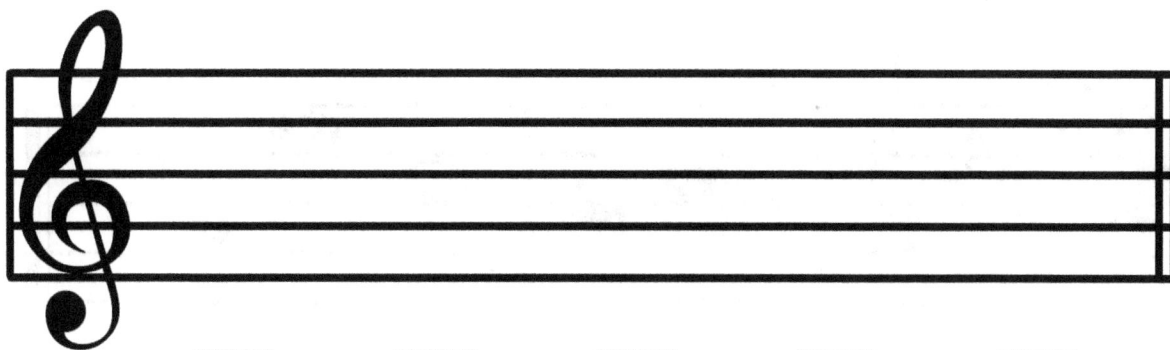

S   L   S   L   S

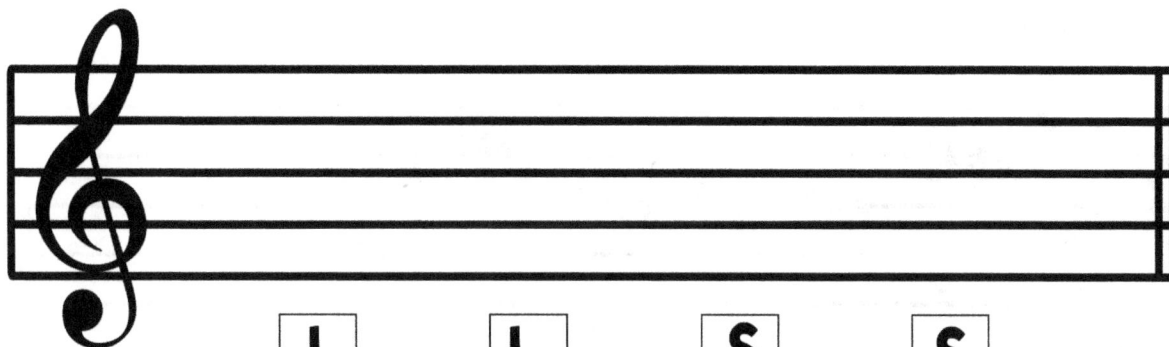

L   L   S   S

PRACTICE BLUES

BASEBALL STRETCH

DESSERT DESIRES

KARATE KICK

SWIM SHARK

FLOATIE FRIEND

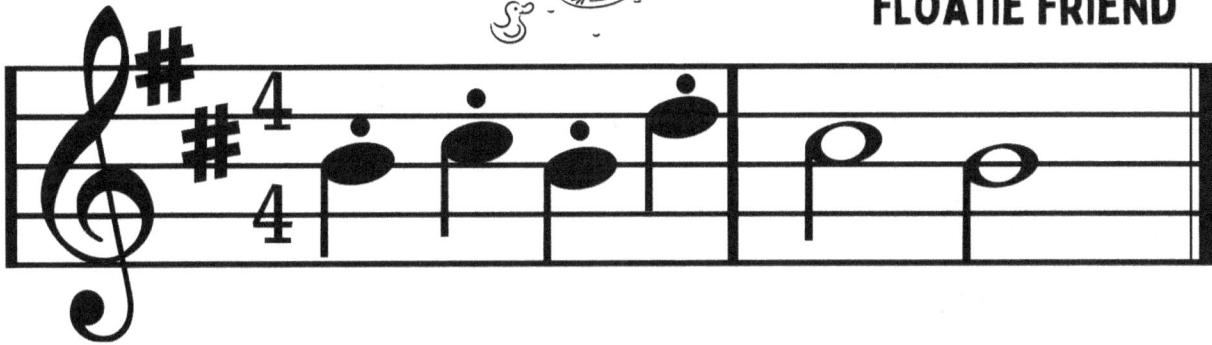

YELLOW BELT

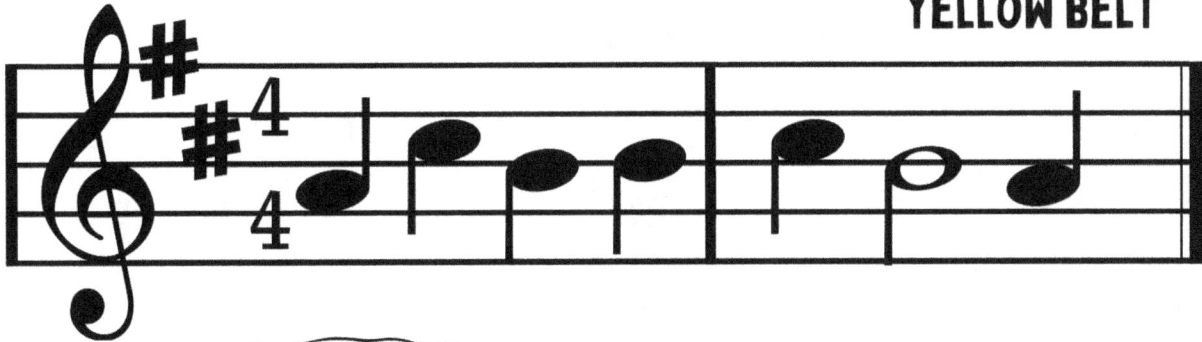

STARRY NIGHT

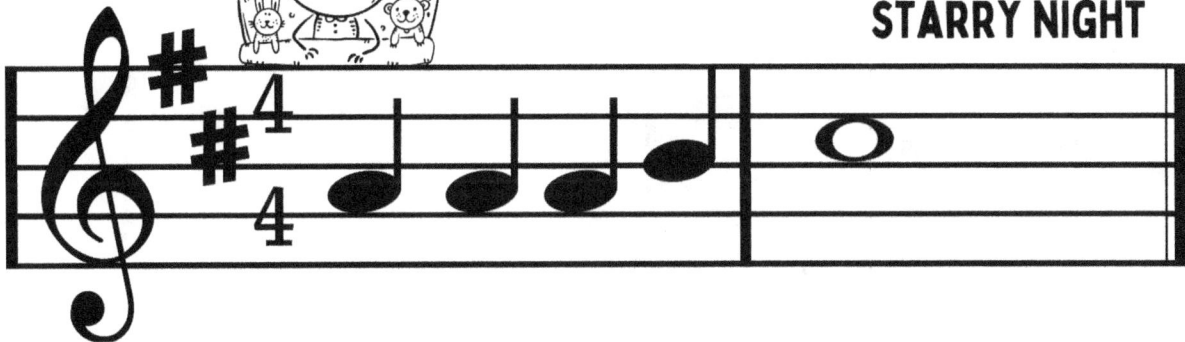

PLAY TIME

I DON'T WAN-NA PRAC-TICE

I JUST WANNA PLAY

MY MOM SAYS I HAFF-TA OR

NO DES-SERT TO-DAY!

DOWN IN THE DUGOUT

PITCH HITTER

JUDY NAILLON

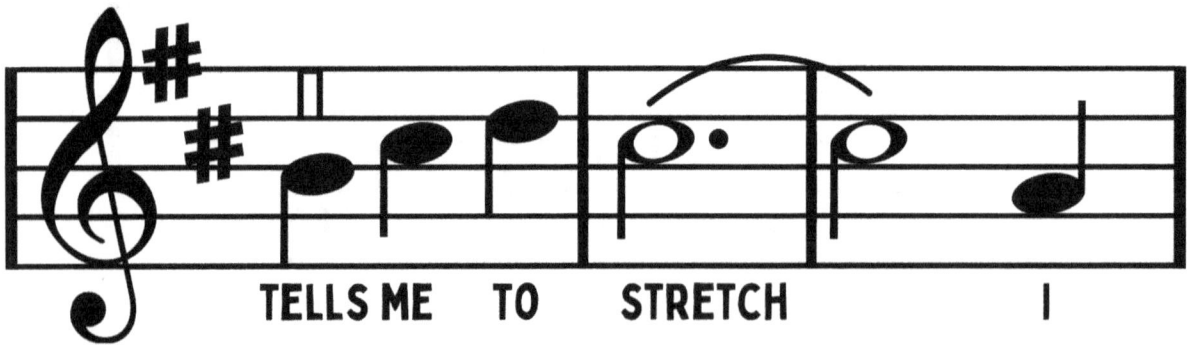

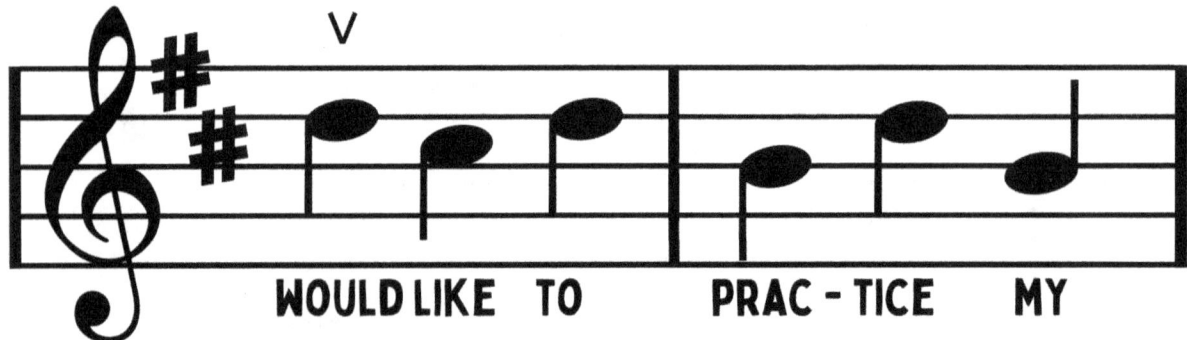

HIT- TING, BUT IN THE OLD

DUG -OUT I SIT!

I`LL HIT I`LL

HIT, JUST PUT ME IN THE LINE UP

1ST ENDING
2ND ENDING

AND I`LL HIT! I WON`T QUIT!

PRACTICE BLUES

"PRACTICE,   PRACTICE,"   THAT'S ALL MY

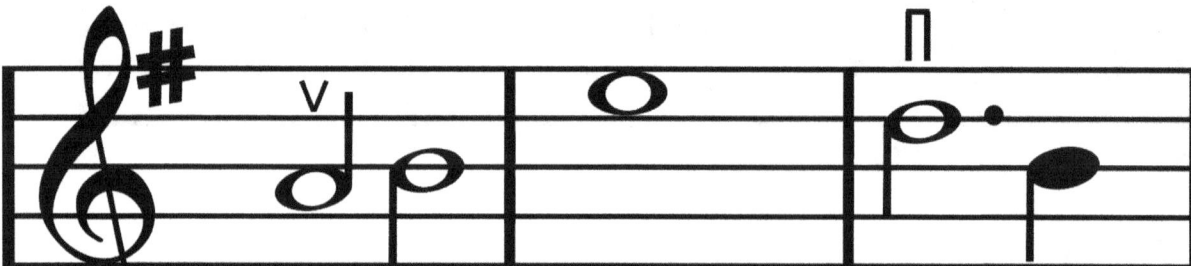

MOM WIL   SAY!   I   ASK

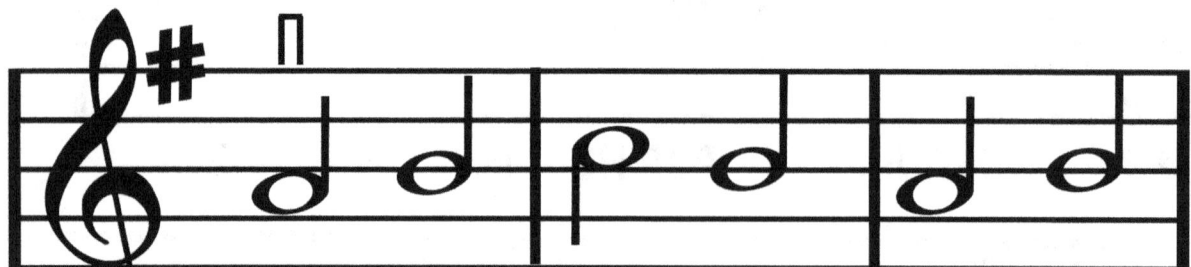

FOR   MY   GAME CON-   TROLL- ER

MOM SAYS   I   CANNOT   PLAY.

I TOLD HER I'LL PRACTICE LA - TER

I'VE GOT IM- PORTANT THINGS TO DO

I WANT TO PLAY GAMES WITH MY BUDDIES,

INSTEAD I'VE GOT THE PRACTICE BLUES!

VIOLIN OPEN A, 1 ON A, 2 ON A

THEORY BLUES

VIOLIN OPEN A, 1 ON A, 2 ON A, 3 ON A

| 2 | 1 | 3 | 0 | |

| | | | |

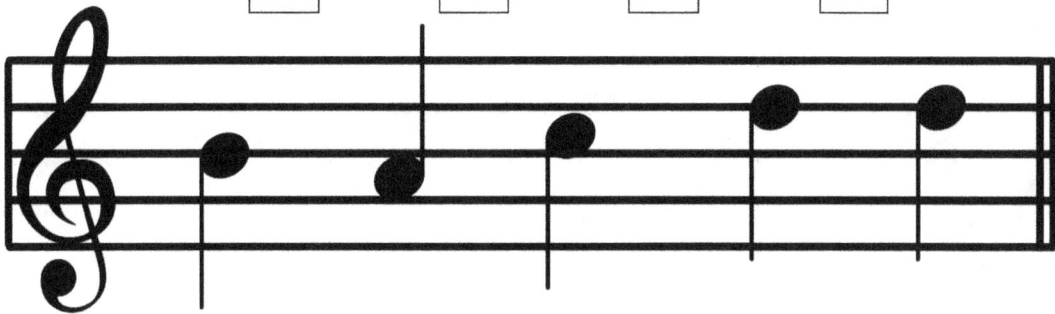

| | | | | |

| | | | |

KARATE KICKS

YOU CAN CHOOSE YOUR OWN BOWING FOR THIS PIECE!

I LOVE TO DO KA-

RAT- E I CAN

JUMP HIGH AND KICK

MOM SIGNED ME UP FOR THESE

LES- SONS I GOT

SICK OF IT QUICK!

I JUST WANT- ED TO

BREAK BOARDS BUT SEN- SEI

SAYS I MUST SIT AND LEARN

HOW TO MASTER THE

BA-SIC HITS, I THINK

I'LL QUIT!

BEAMED 8TH NOTES

THIS IS A BEAM

THIS IS A BALANCE BEAM

WITH THE BEAM NOW
THESE ARE 8TH NOTES

IN MUSIC SOMETIMES NOTES HAVE A BEAM, THIS IS A LINE THAT CONNECTS THE STEMS TOGETHER. THIS IS SECRET CODE FOR FASTER NOTES! BUT HOW MUCH FASTER DO WE PLAY THESE NOTES? TWICE AS FAST AS A QUARTER NOTE. WHEN YOU SEE A QUARTER NOTE THINK "WALK" AND WHEN YOU SEE EITGHTH NOTES THINK "RUNNING"

TO HELP YOU REMEMBER TO PLAY BEAMED NOTES FASTER,
HIGHLIGHT EACH BEAM IN THE
NEXT PIECE WITH YOUR FAVORITE COLOR!

SWIMMING LESSONS

SWIM LESSONS   ARE REALLY CHILLY

THIS POOL'S TOO   COOL.   IT'S NOT MUCH

FUN WHEN I HAVE TO   FOLLOW THESE

RULES: NO   SPLASHING

NO   GOING DOWN THE   WATER SLIDES

TOO!   JUST   SWIM - MING

LAPS BACK AND FORTH TIL   MY TOES TURN

BLUE!

SUMMER BUMMER

THIS SUMMER IS REALLY A

BUM - MER, I JUST WANT TO

PLAY MY GAMES BUT MOM HAS ME

SIGNED UP FOR SO MANY THINGS, THIS

SUMMER IS TOTALLY LAME!

SUMMER SURPRISE

SUMMER'S ALMOST OVER NOW

BUT I HAD A BIG SUR - PRISE

I JUST PITCHED A PERFECT GAME

I MADE SWIM TEAM HALL OF FAME!

IN KA - RA - TE

I KICKED SO MUCH WOOD!

MAY- BE MY MOM

I MIS-UND-ER STOOD!

VIOLIN SQUEAKS

TO - DAY   I   SOUN - DED

BAD,   AND IT   MADE   ME   SO

MAD,   TEACHER   JUST   SAID   "OH

"NO!?",   THEN I   ROS- INED   MY   BOW!

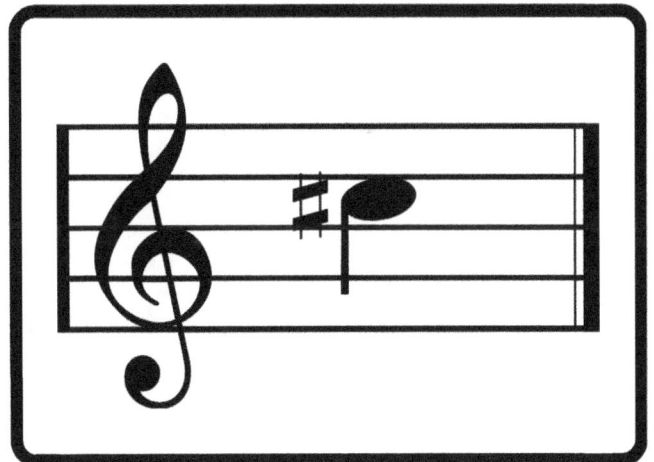

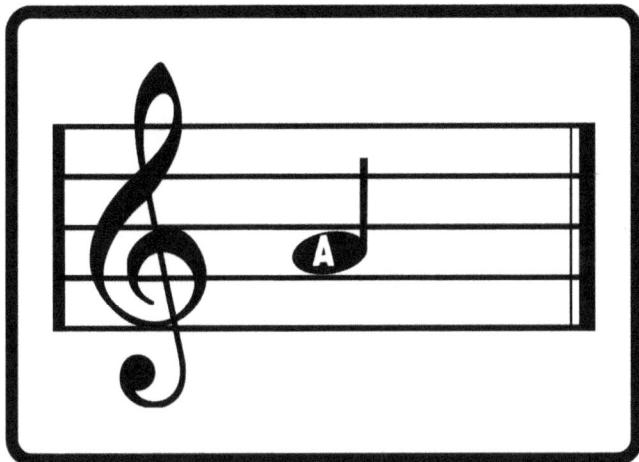

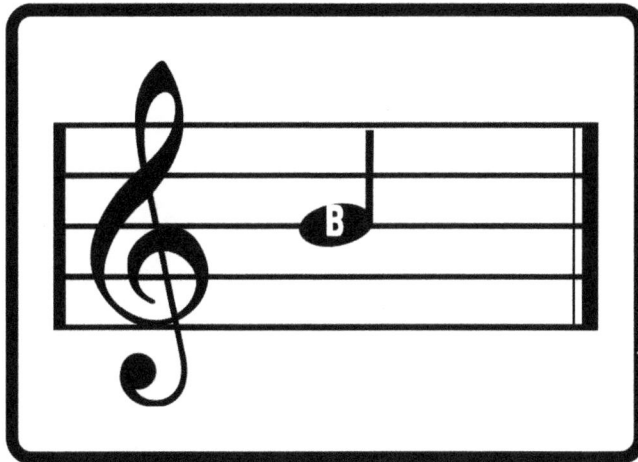

A

B

C

D

E

D

C NATURAL

LOW 2 ON A

C SHARP

HIGH 2 ON A

SET UP YOUR VIOLIN WITH FINGERING TAPES:

Full Size Violin (4/4)
Tape 1 – 35mm (1 3/8 inches)
Tape 2 – 66mm (2 5/8 inches)
Tape 3 – 80mm (3 1/8 inches)
Tape 4 – 106mm (4 1/8 inches)

3/4 Violin
Tape 1 – 32mm (1 1/4 inches)
Tape 2 – 61mm (2 3/8 inches)
Tape 3 – 75 mm (2 7/8 inches)
Tape 4 – 100 mm (3 7/8 inches)

1/4 Violin
Tape 1 – 25mm (1 inch)
Tape 2 – 48mm (1 7/8 inches)
Tape 3 – 60mm (2 3/8 inches)
Tape 4 – 79mm (3 1/8 inches)

1/2 Violin
Tape 1 – 28mm (1 1/8 inches)
Tape 2 – 54mm (2 1/8 inches)
Tape 3 – 68mm (2 5/8 inches)
Tape 4 – 91mm (3 5/8 inches)

You can put a finger tape on your Violin for every finger but you only need two tapes-one for finger #1 in the natural position and one for finger #3. Finger two ALWAYS snuggles up next to finger three in this book. The above chart will help you determine where to place each tape on your specific size violin!
Measure from below the nut -see the above arrow for where to start.

Violin Judy

Mrs. Judy Naillon, or "ViolinJudy" is a dedicated and enthusiastic independent piano and violin teacher, composer, and professional violinist. Her work consists of her large private music studio, as well as playing with her string quartet and Wichita Symphony Orchestra. She served as a church musician for over 20 years and is active in leadership in the musicians' union. She loves coming up with creative ideas to help both students and teachers be successful and blogs about it all at www.ViolinJudy.com and for Alfred's Music Publishers. When she is not writing new Violin books she loves spending time with her family and little dog Pom.

BOOK LEVEL CHART FOR THE **VERY FUN VIOLIN LIBRARY**

VIOLIN GRADE	FUN VIOLIN LEVEL	MAIN CONCEPTS
PRE-TWINKLE	A	RHYTHMS, FINGERS 1,2,3 ON A FINGER 1 ON E
LEVEL 1A	B	NOTE READING 1,2,3 ON A OPEN D & 1 ON E
LEVEL IB	C	NOTE READING ON D, A & E STRINGS, FINGER 4
LEVEL 2A	D	NOTE READING ON ALL STRINGS
LEVEL 2B	E	INTRO TO 3RD POSITION & VIBRATO

CERTIFICATE
OF ACHIEVEMENT

This awarded to :

-- -- -- -- -- -- -- -- -- -- -- -- --

for the achievement of the completion of:

-- -- -- -- -- -- -- -- -- -- -- -- --

_____   _____
Teacher   Date